FINISHING LINE PRESS

www.finishinglinepress.com

Inheritance

poems by

Carla Drysdale

Finishing Line Press
Georgetown, Kentucky

Inheritance

ACKNOWLEDGMENTS

I offer my gratitude to the editors of the following journals where these poems
originally appeared, some in slightly different versions:

"Inheritance" and "Rafael's Question" in *PRISM*
"Sonogram" in *96 Inc.*
"Newborn's Mouth," "Workday," "All Born Perfect," "Leap," "Motherhood Invents
    Me" and "The Next Life" in *The Same*
"Recognition" in *Literary Mama*
"First night in Rougemont" in *Wolf Willow Journal*
"Clemency on the Q Train" in *Weekly Poem*
"The Odds" in *Scapegoat Review*

I am especially grateful to *PRISM* for awarding me the Earle Birney Poetry Prize
for "Inheritance" in May, 2014.

Editor: Christen Kincaid

Cover Art: Ken Dubin, "Origin"

Author Photo: Marcel Crozet

Cover Design: Elizabeth Maines

Printed in the USA on acid-free paper.
Order online: www.finishinglinepress.com
            also available on amazon.com

Author inquiries and mail orders:
Finishing Line Press
P. O. Box 1626
Georgetown, Kentucky 40324
U. S. A.

Table of Contents

for my sons,
David and Rafael

Inheritance

One of my two sons devours books
as I did, bespectacled, silent.

There are childhood facts I'd like to check,
but the past is unpopular

with my mother. Her husband wasn't a reader.
His eye was on me during the day

and at night, when the door opened
and carved a wedge of hall light

into my dark room. I would wait for it.
Her pain was mine when

I heard the hush through the wall
after one of their bedroom fights

and her fall into Valium numbness.
My other son peers into

the legacy behind my eyes,
at what I'm trying to hide.

His pleasure and pain
are always mine

as when he kisses his cat or bends
his pen in half and yells at me,

enraged by the words
on the page.

Dwarf Beech in July

His palomino Champ stood sunlit in the paddock
built by Ray, my stepfather, who swore to make
animals cower like the grey mouse brought in by our
cat last night. Decades ago, my grandparents admired
my girlish penmanship in my letters that left things
out, like the uncertain comfort of the front room
couch, the girl who stayed put beneath her pink
comforter. Ray is dead now. So is the horse and so
is the mouse. On this rainy July day in front of our
house the Dwarf Beech twirls its lime green umbrella
over its elaborately twisted trunk.

The Odds

Even as a child I felt sorry for my father
for his unending hunger, for the wound
reopened every time he picked me up
and dropped me off. Now, nearly fifty
years later, he uses my birth date
for his passwords, as though they
could open a locked door to the past
to when I was small and crawling.
He plays my lucky numbers
on horses and the lottery
but the odds don't change.
Debts still sting like north
Ontario winds of his
boyhood, loneliness,
his father's belt.

Ice Storm in Port Stanley

I remember frozen waves heaved onto sand

We had left the pickup truck nearby
And gone walking, kicking the rough edges
And spikes of ice

We explored the spectacle of water stopped hard
By cold in its tumble to shore
It was like walking
Around a brutal thought before its onslaught
From the tongue

Instead of the conflict we were locked in
We were caught up, swept away
Hands frozen, breath steaming
Below a metallic sky, by something
The man called "dad"
And I were awed by.

Giving Up on Revenge

Would you feel sorry for my husband, Ray,
just because he married me?
I'm the girl you resented having to raise.
At nights my sheets were territory
mapped by our battle over who had the right
to own me. You already possessed my mother.
Back then I was ten. I was your goods. I lost that fight.
Who says the dead and living can't talk to each other?
Though you're beyond the grave and I'm still here
you're as close as the feeling of falling into
the thin place between forgiveness and fear.
Did anyone ever feel sorry for you?
I wish to surrender my right to avenge
for the sake of my children becoming men.

Sonogram

None of us carries the life we intended.
My body's core holds a stranger to me
unborn and unaware of a mother
alive with the howling of unmet needs
passed from one generation to another
like pictures from unbearable dreams
that demand to be uncovered and seen.

Miscarriage

High summer. The day
is hot, harrowed, hallowed.

"Nature is a terror,"
the doctor said.

Gray needles cluster
like stars

on branches of the Blue Atlas Cedar
in the community garden.

Manhattan traffic roars alongside
a screen of laurel

vine debris rains
on me like green confetti.

The Braid

First, my cry, then yours, split the sky
above that Brooklyn hospital
as you, limbs curled and purple
slid out of my body
after a prolonged and irreversible journey.
Pain, then
absence of pain.

The midwife held you up,
infant boy, alive in this world.
You peed an arc of urine
sparkling over the bed
and over her.

The champagne cork popped,
we all drank to life
you suckled on a nipple
lips still rimmed
with watery blood from that
other life inside.

We lay together, suspended,
holding on to each other.
Tough braid of blue and red
still binding us
cut for the first and last time.

Newborn's Mouth

Breath the scent of apple slice
freshly cut sickle moon.

Tiny cavern of ridges and gums,
dark receiver of my aureole, nipple, milk.

His mouth
pulls the blue-white silk thread

from my body to his
knitting a blanket for us to curl up in

until his howl
and the next unraveling.

Recognition

He'd been crying.
Now, I'm back.
His mouth, overflowing
with breast milk, drips over
my stomach, when he stops
sucking to look at me, relieved.
Shamelessly happy.

The way new lovers
stop kissing for a moment
just to look at each other
still shocked to have found
each other, and now
to be held, to behold!

The way I used to give myself
over and over to strangers.
It was always worth it.
Even if I was used and rejected.

Workday

Morning's the whine and clunk
of the elevator stopping on our floor.
My key turns, locks the door. As I run
for the bus I don't know

when I'll die
nor how dyslexia will affect
my son's life or which way
my marriage will go. At work

I remember the mineral smell
of my other son's scalp under
his nap of closely cropped hair.

In bed each evening I don't hear
sleep's wing beats as I drift
into houses over fields, oceans

I don't hear the crack and roar
of melting polar ice, smell earth's
openings as it warms

can't feel the tides
rising and rising.

Chore

My mother
waits again for
me to get
in the car
leave it all
God is good
I've forgotten
again
telling things
smelling the rich
honky-tonk song
she wore
to cover herself
pitching horse shit

Never understood
why I had to write
the truth
go to church
to God
to stay alive
to come home
drunk on words, wine
I've written about
animal scent
mother's purple suede coat
like a mantle
all those pre-dawn mornings
in the barn

All Born Perfect

Objects of my life
strewn across this table,
laid down in the precision of words:
green apples from a basket,
notebook and pen,
what I will say
and what I won't.

The old sorrow--
the one that won't go away
no matter how much
talking, pills, sex, wine,
even vengeance--
has become a blind dog now
its snout resting on paws.
Rilke said the dragons of fear
really just want our love.

The old sorrow remains
despite the distractions and good news
and good weather.
Even my children don't erase it.
Instead they gather
new ones for themselves
they imagine no one else carries,
all born perfect with howling needs.

Does anything change?
I have gone away to motherhood
and in that place where mothers stood
there is silence.

"You will write again," said Stanley Kunitz
in my dream.
"You will speak
in a green voice
you hardly recognize."

Fierce

At the Toys R Us in Kingston, New York,
my son chooses a sword.

Not yet five, he knows
a sword is more
than a weapon for settling scores.

He chooses the most ancient-looking one
for its shiny metallic plastic,

for the twin dragons,
intertwined
as one thought at the hilt,
fierce furl, unfurling,

for the gold handle crafted
to command the universe.

After I pay for it, we walk out
to the concrete parking lot
where his father and younger brother
wait in the car for us.

It is spring. Lush mountains surround us.
My son lances and the world
bounces off his blade, in which
I see flashes of his face
and my own.

Rare

Pushing your stroller
to bucket swings at Sixteen Sycamores
we are stopped by a woman
who calls you a rare bird.

Everyone, including her,
wants to touch your hair
which looks copper-fired.

I am so tired in this first haze of motherhood,
I smile and say thank you
while you giggle in your eighth month.

Both of us take this moment for granted.
We can't live every moment lit by love itself.

Water Boys

My two boys sit still, for once,
at the Brooklyn Museum, entranced
by the video of a man's quest for water.

Two buckets in hand, he leaps down
two steps at a time to the truck's spigot
returns to an apartment six flights up
to the top of a decrepit complex
in crumbling, hot Cuba.

Over and over, he empties and refills
the buckets until he's almost falling down.

Finally, he strips off his shorts,
steps into the brown enamel tub
and sinks slowly until only mouth and nose
rest above the water line
his lips pulled back by his beatific smile.

My boys sit still,
silent as the taste of water.

Leap

This evening I linger in their room
longer than usual, resist my impulse to get out,
away from them, to peace and privacy.
Instead I yield to the buttery
nightlight shadows.

My hand scratches his lean, bare back.
When he says, "Mom, move your fingers
apart," there's a little leap in me,
glad he knows how to ask, as we lie there
precisely for what he wants.

Labyrinth

She who bore me, supported my slack newborn neck
in her palm while she bathed me in a small basin,
warm water tested on her wrist

She who smoothed the auburn down of my brow, laundered
cotton diapers and stacked them four feet high
so she'd have enough

She who led me up and down stairs, whose hand meant home.
Who tickled freckles at bedtime as I sank,
sighing, into pillows.

She who ran cold vinegar baths for my sunburned skin.
Who covered me up in the sun, but neglected the darkness
I was in, in the garage

where her husband hussied me. Her voice made books
breathe while I held my tongue – *Don't tell* –
my secret burning still,

long after her escape from him, leaving me as well.
Abandonment, it sounds so harsh, then and now,
well, doesn't it?

I still can't find her in the labyrinth of denial, and I envy
those who seem to live as though their mother never
existed, living or dead.

Insomnia

When you left, mother,
at first I was numb.
Then feeling came back

as panic, little black feathers
folding softly over my mouth.
Still, sometimes, waking at 3 am

from star-darkness of sleep,
breathing lightly
in my creaturely self

questions wing
under ancient scar-stars:
Why did you go?

Why didn't I go with you?
How my past stays alive
under your plumage.

The Gaze

Her pony-tailed daughter,
I stand in the kitchen
pouring another glass of red wine.
She waits to be served
at my table now. Turning,
I catch my mother
looking at me, into me,
as if the lamp-lit moment itself
could reveal to her
who I am and where I've gone.
I pretend not to notice,
turn and rinse another glass.

Often, I drink in my boys'
four and six year-old faces
while they stare at the TV screen.
Since they're distracted
I can gorge
on their almond eyes,
chocolate and hazel;
their honey blonde and auburn heads.
I can't stop gazing at them
in the same way
she can't fold away
her longing.

Motherhood Invents Me

Under house arrest and tired to my marrow.
I bend down, again, to clean up their mess.
My anger a tire iron.
Two young sons, ruby-lipped, hair shining, want what I want.
Food, play, and the sleep of dreams.
To be told I'm good.
But I can't go back to that life, before them.
It brought me here.

First night in Rougemont

*"And the future holds the most remote event
in union with what we most deeply want."*
(Rainer Maria Rilke, from the Sonnets to Orpheus)

Standing in pine-scented wind
I am lit by full moon's opalescence.
Church bells toll a full fifteen minutes.

Stained by October's alpine shadows
I lift my too-full wine glass to the axis
of church, moon and mountaintop.

Inside, my children bask
in TV screen's hypnotic light
despite my calls to step into the chiming night.

When I open the door, they yell "no"
pull the duvet to their chins
a shield against the cold.

You see, they want their story
and I want mine.
Though we live each other's.

So I stand alone
watching mist from the valley rising
like persistent and prodigal longing.

The Next Life

Could I come back as a tree?
A Blue Atlas cedar
with star clusters for needles.
Wind, pale and blue,
bear my seeds to new
ground. Use bird beak,
insect and squirrel.
From here, that pine
leans like a torch song.
Sway, branch, sway.
Who wouldn't want that height,
those roots, that heft?
The silken spikes.

Clemency on the Q Train

A bee large as my thumb
turns in circles
on the black rubber floor
flecked with star speckled pattern
like outer space or a pebbled shore
under our feet
as the Q train rumbles home.

Silent subway riders
watch the bee lumber up
and stumble across the blue
and white checkerboard
of a large tennis shoe

"Step on it!" someone says.
But I'll tell you quickly
he doesn't kill.

Awkwardly, gently, the shoe
nudges the bee
out into the clear space
between platform edge
and sliding door.

Hunkered

My father brings in sagging boxes
softened by years
stacked in storage, waiting for me.

Now they hunker on the living
room floor of his bachelor
apartment this hot day.

My sons and their dad escape
to a translucent pool while I rip open
box after box.

I find books mostly, with advice
on becoming a writer, plus diaries, cards,
articles I'd written for trade magazines,
a few college essays, high school
year books. Love letters to and from
people I'd be uncomfortable

around now. My hair is heavy, curling
with humidity as I lean into the late
afternoon dust.

Words slide through my
grimy hands. Thankful my fingertips
are blind, I salvage only enough

for a carry-on. My father tries
to recapture lost time, talking to me
about his life and loneliness

the color of faded lottery tickets.
I can't remember my mother and him
ever being together.

My kids and husband reappear, smelling
of coconut sunscreen and chlorine. They pick
through things: a cedar box with a key,

my amateur still-life drawings
which they insist we keep. My father
will deal with what we leave behind.

Rafael's Question

My son carries the name
of the healing archangel. He

sits on my lap, at the computer's
luminous screen. We look at photos

of my parents, divorced
when I was two. Their faces

sagging, eyes hopeful.
Still alive, but their visits to us

number less than a handful
in his five-year-old life.

Sometimes, after brushing our teeth
he'll say, "Mom, make it like a river."

And I'll cup my palms together
under running water, and he'll drink.

Tonight as we sit together
I'm silent, because it's hard to explain.

He asks, "Do you still love them?"
So gently, so gently.

Additional Acknowledgments

And for these people, without whom the poems would never have been completed, I am grateful: Molly Peacock, sustaining mentor and poetry mother; Carolyn Forché for guiding me to new places in poetry; John Glenday for his good eye and encouragement; the Mutual Muses (Julia Shipley, Cindy Frenkel, Janet Read, and Laura Sillerman) for nudging me forward; the Geneva Writers Group and writers Claudia Spahr, Elizabeth Coleman, Susan Jane Gilman and Anne Korkeakivi; Anne Marie Macari for believing in this work, and the poets at the Colrain Poetry Manuscript Conference for revision help. Loretta Hieber-Girardet, Julie Flood-Hunt and Marion Canute, thanks for bolstering my confidence over the years. To Kasey Jueds, profound thanks for your ever deepening friendship and poetic insight. To Sharon Guskin, your love and wisdom remind that "there is no perfect, special or shame," and I am grateful. Thank you Jonathan for everything you do and feel, for continuing to nurture me with food, music and laughter and for loving our sons and me. To David and Rafael, thank you for making me your mother. It is a lifetime privilege and adventure.

The following places offered the shelter and silence I needed to enter the space of these poems: The Virginia Center for the Creative Arts, The Convent of St. Helena in New York, the Abbaye de la Fille-Dieu in Romont, Switzerland and the Hôtellerie Foyer Franciscain in Saint Maurice, Switzerland.

To the team at Finishing Line Press, Leah Maines, Christen Kinkaid and Elizabeth Maines, thank you for loving these poems enough to make this book. Thanks to Marcel Crozet for my author photo and for the gorgeous painting used on the cover, I am indebted to artist Ken Dubin.

Carla Drysdale is a Canadian poet who lives in France just over the border from Geneva, where she works as an editor, writer and communications consultant. She lives with her husband and two boys.

Her poems have appeared in numerous publications, including Cleaver Magazine, Scapegoat Review, Zoetic Press, *PRISM, The Same, LIT, the Literary Review of Canada, Canadian Literature, The Fiddlehead, Global City Review, Literary Mama* and in the anthology *Entering the Real World: VCCA Poets on Mt. San Angelo.* In May, 2014 she was awarded PRISM's annual Earle Birney poetry prize for her poem, "Inheritance." Her poem, "New Year's Eve" was set to music by American composer David Del Tredici.

Her first full-length collection of poems, *Little Venus,* was published by Toronto's Tightrope Books in 2009.

She received an MFA in Poetry from Sarah Lawrence College in 1999 and has been awarded residencies at the Virginia Center for the Creative Arts and La Porte Peinte in Noyers-Sur-Serein, France.

Writing poetry is her lifelong quest towards wholeness and connection with the natural world and with others.

www.ingramcontent.com/pod-product-compliance
Lightning Source LLC
LaVergne TN
LVHW091234080426
835509LV00009B/1281